ANALYZE PEOPLE

Analysis of human behavior through the use
of body language and manipulation, secret
techniques to read people, recognize lies
and mind control

FRIEDRICH LLOYD

Table of Contents

Introduction

This book will look into the subject of analyzing people. Analyzing people is a different dimension and a hectic process in which the person's mind and character are discussed. What are the successive attributes of the person and how that person is able to shape his statements and modes of socialization in any situation? The process of dealing with the human mind is all about analysis and this book will deeply decipher the constructs of analysis properly.

Human behavior will be properly studied. Human behavior is a complex term, in which the values, norms and social orders are deeply considered for the benefit of human behavior. Human behavior precisely deals with this assertion of how people are able to manifest a strong token of appreciation for others and how does this behavior changes with respect to time. For example, according to

Montesquieu (1992), human behavior changes with time and in order to make a proper understanding of human behavior, one has to deeply socialize with the subject. Therefore, human behavior is a complex term that tends to make the aspiration of a human engine complete and with this interesting project, the behavior of the human will be periodically discussed.

The importance of body language is yet another topic that will be needing clarification in this book. Body language refers to the use of words, language slogans, language terminologies and language instructs through which the person is able to resonate a strong mode of conviction to others. In terms of other ways, body language is tantamount to proper resonation in the home atmosphere. Body language will always make the human people understand the concept of uniformity in the making and with the passage of time, the people are able to have a strong mode of communication with other people. Body language can be made easy if the person uses a certain amount of tactics through which the body language is deeply affected. These tools will be discussing in brevity in the following pages and there will be a potent use of clarification for other personalities. Thus, the use of body language will enable the person to make the system go way much better.

Reading and detecting people will also be illustrated in this method. The people will understand the primary concepts of people to people analysis that people garner the use of body language for their benefits. These all terms will be carefully discussed in this book and emphasis will be given to the concept of reading the minds of others.

Chapter 1 Basic Concepts

This chapter will deal with the basic concepts that are affiliated with analyzing people. It will throw light on approaches to human behavior, the definition of human behavior and the prediction of human behavior. The ideas will be coherent in this regard and a lot of emphases will be given to the term human analysis.

Human Behavior

Human behavior has interpreted a kind of behavior in which a human is perceived in a social, economical and logical context. The behavior starts to evolve from babyhood to adolescence and it has many impacts on it. The babyhood method is used to see the nature and nurture of the baby, through which he is able to attain a strong reservation in the prospects of life. The human behavior of youth is dependent on three modes. The first mode if of cultural progression. Under what culture, the human is able to grow and how the culture impacts the gender of the human is all that cultural progression is about. In this phase, the cultural ingredients that are the role of economics, religion, politics and society are carefully discussed. This cultural progression is able to garner most of the capabilities of the people and with the passage of time, the public is able to transform the ideas of human behavior effectively. Therefore, cultural progression is a valid argument, which gives brief institutions to work holistically.

The second mode is cognitive development in which the people are able to be interpreted in the construct of small and large cognition holistically. The cognition comes with respect to time and the person is interpreted according to cognition. This means that more the person thinks, the cognition process wants to be established effectively and with the passage of time, the people are able to have more insight into this respective issue.

So, cognition development is a process through which a person's mind is actually construed and with the process of time and phase, he is understood to be a human.

The third mode is of gender development. By gender development, it is asserted the evolutionary phases, that the person is able to integrate into his or her character through the passage of time, is referred to be as gender development. Gender development is a strong process through which both men and women learn effectively. The men ratio is all about rage and individualistic opinion while the women want to be more progressive and expressive in their nature. Therefore, they tend to mold the constructs of their behavior and with the passage of time, the people are able to have more inclination to the coming time. Thus, the use of gender development is important to be understood in a pragmatic manner.

So, these are three modes of human development and these modes are able to be effective in the coming mode of time due to which they are able to have more generic comprehensions in their making. This concept is more aggressive in its demand and it can demand many overtures in its coming phase.

Theories of Human development

This portion of the chapter will deal strongly with the constructs of human development in which the person is able to have strong modes of comprehension with the public. These theories will be developed by eminent philosophers and scientists in the coming time. The individual that use these kinds of behavior were Sigmund Freud, Charles Darwin and many more. Their theories along with their comprehensions are as follows:

Sigmund believed that every person is born with a notion known as libido. This libido is tantamount to the emotional development of the child and the child is able to harness the emotional development of libido and thus, with the passage of time, he develops the aspirations of love and adoration. The aspiration is more systematic in their nature and the child learns the wrongs and rights of life. This libido makes the child more pragmatic in its nature and the child can delve into many aspirations in later life. The child learns the love matters with the mom of the family, he tends to be more affiliated with the opposite gender and there is a sense of authorization of the person with the family member. Therefore, the construction of libido is a concept, which is more effective for people to learn it holistically. The idea is simple in its regard and hence the people are able to make the inclinations in it with respect to time.

Freud also developed a structure of personality for the people. The people are able to have a strong mode of reservation with the other modes of society. Freud believed that every person has its own sense of longing with other personalities and the personalities change with respect to time. The time of personality development is able to induce people with more and more assertions with respective time. The time table of the person varies with strong conservations and the person is able to have more evolution in the coming time. Therefore, the personality assessment of the person is able to be achieved with respect to time. Freud believed that in order to have a strong goal in personality development, one needs to harbor subjectivity in its core relations. The subjectivity could come with respect to time and the person can learn through it. If the subjectivity is all minimum and the person is not able to have enough interactions with the people then there is no usage of a strong personality. The personality orders will deplete with respect of time and the person would not be able to make hard assertions in the coming time. Thus, the personality assessment needs to be checked while catering to the making of a personality and Freud believes that it is an important way to check the balances of the person in the coming time.

Erick Erikson was also of the belief of how people can be elevated in the construct of emotional belief. He believed that people are able to have sound knowledge on the topic of assertion and personality making. However, the situations in the coming time are quite different. Erik wanted the person to have an emotional check on them through which many people, will be able to have sound careers in the book. The idea is that the person is not able to make sound assertions in the coming time. He believed that the person must have an emotional character making in the time and this will help them to make the issues to make more interesting and capable in the coming time. Therefore, Erick will make you believe that the person will be able to induce more progression in the coming time.

Erik had eight stages of development for the human. These are: infancy, trust versus mistrust, early childhood, preschool and school age. He believed that the person is able to learn a lot through these days and with the passage of time, the person is able to have a strong check on his mind as well. These eight stages govern the body language as well as the human behavior of the individual in a coherent manner. The trust versus mistrust is a mindset and a process in which the child is able to learn the major advantages of socialization and ideas that who to trust and who not to. The trust factor comes with the process of time and it helps the individual to learn many ground realities of the time and human behavior. Therefore, it is important to understand how the public is able to be shamed by the narrative of human development.

Another scientist in this educational venture is Piaget, who belongs to Switzerland and he is able to make the mobilities of the personality a bad place. He wants to study the intellectual functioning and reasoning of the individual that how the person is able to have strong intellectual cognition with a person in an effective manner. The effect of the cognition is so sound and great that the person is able to carve out a personal space of livelihood to other personalities in the coming time. The cognition helps to have a systematic endeavor in the coming time and therefore, a person is able to have a strong impact on its personality with the coming time. Thus, cognition is a side to a person's ability with which he is able to make a strong inclination in the person's mind. Hence, it is important for you to understand that why the person is not able to have a strong grip on intellectual freedom and this is exactly a thesis that Mr. Piaget is able to develop with the passage of time.

Next comes the contextualization of learning theory. This is the theory that advocates the sum of all the construction of humans in the coming time. This theory asserts the possibility of strong cognition and mobility in the coming time and any person, who has a strong sense of living is able to have a concentrated pillar of extractions in the coming time. The learning theory is able to make sound credentials in the coming time. This theory helps individuals to make reasons for living and adopting free in the coming time. The people want to make the credence of the personalities more functioning in the coming time and according to them, the person is able to have a sense of pleasure if all its learning and progression are learned in an effective manner. The idea here is not that the person is not able to make strong contention in the coming time but he is sure of dealing with the person float in an effective manner. This sense of actualization comes in the person when he is learning and hence, learning theory helps to deal with the person more effectively and holistically.

So, these are some of the theories, spearheaded by political scientists that can lead to the comprehension of the public. Human development is a complex manner, which is able to be perceived collectively by humans and humans tend to resolve more contextualization for human development. These theories will help to resolve the function come in a generic way and the person will understand effectively the constructs of the individual in a standard manner. Therefore, human development is a process that is able to have a strong generalization of the instruments in a cool manner. The idea is simply that one needs to be well functioning and adaptable in its current outlook and in order to have more strong ingredients of human development, one also needs to form strong approaches to it. Thus, the next section of the book will deal with the incisive approaches which help us understand the mode of human development easily.

Approaches to Understand Human Behavior

There are five major approaches to understand human behavior.

1. The Psychodynamic Approach

The psychodynamic approach was propounded by Sigmund Freud in which he believed that there are three personalities that develop the approach of the person. One is the development of the illness factor. This factor was discovered in the year 1993, when Freud was able to discuss the advantages of the illness emanating of the child. This theory was further comprehended with the passage of time and the people believed that it was able to make the functionalities of the personality look better. Another theory was about the conscious and the subconscious manner. This theory believed that people are able to delve into the personalities of the person in an effective manner. The conscious mind is the mind that is aware of all the pros and cons of living. Whereas, the subconscious mind is the mind, which heralds some of the important aspirations of daily life. According to Freud, the subconscious mind clearly stores a lot of information in the minds of the public and with the passage of time, the person is able to have a strong version of interest in it. The idea of the construction is quite similar to the game because the psychodynamic approach will give you strong comprehension about the functioning of the mind. The system will thereby make you believe in it and with the passage of time, you will be able to have a stronghold on the construction effectively. Therefore, the psychodynamic approach helps you to psychologically listen to the minds of the people and understand them effectively.

2. Behavioral Approach

This is a kind of approach which makes the behaviors of other people understandable through experiences and external stimulus. By many psychologists it is also referred to as the classical conditioning method and the conditioning is done by altering the external stimulus of the public. The public gets to know the major ingredients of the development of behaviorism and with the passage of time, the people get to know the true nature of all the components of real life. The idea is simple and straight here that to make sure that how the people are able to have more strategic interest in their coming, the behavioral approach is possibly maintained and implemented. Therefore, the behavioral approach is an approach, which needs to be strengthened by all means and it tends to give strong reservations in the coming time. So, the reason for making the humans look more understandable and adjustable, the people must not make the hectic decision of life and try its best in making the reasons go way bound.

Predicting Human Behavior

The human behavior of humans can be predicted in the following ways.

The use of Homecourt

This is the manipulation technique in which the individual uses his or her home as an advantage for his own benefits. The psychological demeanor was used to define the crux of the people, who were under the liability of the people. For the substantiation of this case, it is important to understand that the people, who are in a psychological condition to manipulate others are very smart. The first rule is that the public must come into consideration of the psychological master and then the master will navigate his thoughts. First and foremost, the master uses the court to manipulate the personalities and then the public first advocates the use of manipulation to be just and obscure.

Establishing the stance first and then looking for weaknesses

In the manipulation of psychology, it is important to understand that the establishment of the stance is first. The stance needs to be manifested first and then it is established so that the people, who are listening to the track come under the way of the manipulator. Once the stance of the manipulator is established then the maneuvering is very easy. The people have to understand the use of the stance easily and then they have to use the words of the manipulator as a source of manipulation. The people can easily be thrown into the abyss when the manipulator asks a lot of questions. The idea is that the public first navigates the stance and then the manipulator can use the stance to find its justification. If the manipulator wants to find the essence of the stance and if he finds some distortion of the stance then he can avoid the crux of the stance very badly.

Manipulation of Facts

If you want to assert the significance of the psychology of manipulation, then the facts stated can be used to deceive. The facts can be of any statement and that can be used to defy the logic of the people. For instance, if the manipulator is using the fact sound of one thing then that thing can be used to defy as well. People that can assess the logic of the personalities can manipulate by navigating them through their own lies. This is the act of manipulation if people are using the effects of deviance in an effective manner.

Overwhelming with facts and statistics

First and foremost, the fact and statistics can be used to defy the personalities of the public. The facts are to be constructed in an effective manner so that the manipulator can be used to defy the odds of manipulation. So, for a strong manipulation, you have to overwhelm the facts and statistics with the people. The people can be used to come under the clout of statistics if the public is not able to use a strong mode of psychological messages. Therefore, it is important that psychology can be used to interpret the essence of the public in a logical manner.

Overwhelming with procedures and Red tape

In order to maintain the crux of other personalities, the manipulator uses procedures and red tapes to give more defying reasons to the public. The manipulator will use the procedural versions, in which the public has to be manipulated in a stringent manner. The manipulator can be harnessed in a strong way so that the public can give concrete methods to it. For this reason, to be constructed, the manipulator uses some procedures and advantages through which the normal public comes into oppression. This oppression is used to defy the lands of the public and the public comes under the manipulation of the manipulator. So, in order to manipulate the people, the psychologists can use the crux of procedures and some secretive tapes that can be used in a strong manner.

Raising the voice and Displaying Negative Emotions

The manipulator in order to make the voice of the public effective has to raise the voice of himself. The manipulator uses some strong means and modes through which he is able to forecast a shadow of darkness. This darkness is used to construct the methods of manipulation among the stakeholders and the people can come under effective modes of destruction. Also, the negative emotions, give the value of harsh realities among the public and they get severely neglected by the personalities. Therefore, it is important to understand that the public is not able to get manipulated if they see the raised level of voice and hence there is a display of festering emotions among the people.

Negative Surprises

The negative surprises are another mode of manipulation by the manipulator. The manipulate can be using harsh negative surprises through which the people are not able to understand their nature. These negative surprises also affect the effects of the mentality of the public and with the passage of time, the people do not get easily comfortable in this essence. The negative surprises show a strong moment of disinterest among the public and there is a culture of disassociation among the public through the negative surprises. The negative surprises give a sense of bad omens for the public through which the people are not able to give standard modes of deviation for the public.

Giving you a little or no time to decide

The time that has been given to you is either less time or there is no time. The manipulator wants to get his thing done because only then he is effective in his mode. The manipulator would cast his own means to come in front of the public. The time that has been slotted for the manipulator has a strong version of connectedness with the people and thus, there needs to be a strong sense of affection for the people. Therefore, the time of decision that has been given to you is a tool of the manipulator so that the public is able to give more directions for the public. So, the time has to be a motive interest for the public to understand in an effective manner.

Use of Negative Humor

The negative humor is a manipulating tool to disassociate you from your being. The manipulator would cast negative humor on you and will do his best to make you feel bad about the situation. This manipulation is further designed by the manipulator to disempower you and with its continuous bolstering, the use of negative humor could be very harsh and brutal for you. Therefore, the use of negative humor could be used to induce isolationism and fanaticism in public and could be very pernicious for you as well. If the use of negative humor could be bad for you then manipulation could be a stringent maneuver to showcase in-effectiveness among you.

Consistent Judgement

The consistent judgment could be a harsh tactic to induce fright among you. The manipulator could use the essence of judgement to make you feel discomfort able.

How it can be done? This is as follows: Suppose, you are sitting in a room and the manipulator is sitting in front of you and you are able to hear the statements of the manipulator and with the passage of time, the public is not able to define the essence of the judgments properly. The public is quite effective in harboring the essence of the manipulator and if the manipulator is successful is dissing you with his judgments then finally you are under his claw. The consistent judgment will make you feel very demotivated and with the passage of time, you will be feeling delusional.

Silent Treatments

When the manipulator wants to harbor his mechanism then he uses the edifice of silence. This silence is very haunting. It is very managerial and with the passage of time, it induces a bad version of manipulation among you. You get affected by the silence of the manipulator and in time, this becomes very pestering among you. The silent treatment is also very haunting at an individualistic level because at times, the public is not able to see the results of it in a discomforting manner. Therefore, silent treatments can be used to haunt the premises of the individual in a bad manner.

Thus, these are some of the mechanisms that make the prediction of human behavior look way too easy. Therefore, human development needs to be adopted with the passage of time properly.

Chapter 2 Body Language

This chapter will give heed to the concept of body language. The important contents along with their clarifications are as follows:

Importance of Body Language

The body language gives you strong commitments and strong waves of confidence in you. The following are some of the ways that can make body language important for you.

Body Language can generate compassion for you

Just imagine that your shoulders are way too back, the smiles are apparent on your face, the stomach in of yours and the strong eye contact; all these features are important for you and with the passage of time, you will realize that you will be able to induce a spirit of confidence in you and with this confidence, you can make a lot of efforts to the human development and can make the analysis an important way for the public to come on. Therefore, body language can generate compassion for you.

Hand gestures representing yourself

In anybody's language, the use of hand gestures is able to give a sounding impact to the listeners. With strong gestures, the people are able to have pertinent soundings in their constructs and the people are able to infuse meticulous planning in their formation. The idea is simple in this sense because the more you use hand gestures, the more you are able to make healthy developments in the scenario. Therefore, hand gestures are an important tool for you to use in a conversation.

Having a sustainable conversation

The more you use actions in a body language with your tongue and body, the more sustainable conversation you will intend to have. It depends on what is the mechanism of the body language and how this mechanism is able to make you different in any conversation. If you are shy and a little hysterical while conversing, then the conversation would not last long. However, if you tend to be a little more convincing then the conversation will last for long. The idea is simply that you need to have a strong momentum of conversation in your dialogue and with the passage of time, you will develop yourself much better. Hence, the importance of body language is all reflected in your domains in the coming time.

Have an open posture

The use of an open posture is a tool to construct the language portion of the personality. It gives its importance in the construction of humble words and you must be able to have an open posture while you are making yourself more confident and reliable in any conversation. The more you are able to have an open posture, the more you can seduce the personalities with your body language. Therefore, before speaking always have an open posture, due to which you will be able to be joined by other people effectively. Hence, the idea of an open posture starts with strong conversation and impact and you are able to make stringent mechanisms in time.

Speaking without Words

This part of the chapter will tell you that your postures and eye contacts can speak effectively and proverbially for others while you are about to start a conversation. It has the following contents of its clarification.

The use of firm handshake

The more firm is your handshake, the more impact you are able to give to the audience or the people with whom you want to speak. The people judge your mentality when they shake hands with you and they are able to perceive you directly once you are able to have proper handshaking with your friends.

For instance, you want to a bar, the friends at their have a token of interest for you and they tend to give you strong assertions before a conversation. In such a situation, it is quite better to have a strong mode of conversation with the use of a firm handshake. This gesture will deploy hundreds of ways to make you feel much better and proactive in the coming time. Therefore, it is always important to start a conversation with someone, using a handshake.

Maintaining good eye contact

The maintenance of good eye contact is another strong feature of you to make good eye contact. It is not necessary that you are not speaking with anyone but it is highly important for you to have stern contact with others while having a conversation. This gesture would seem as if you are able to give a sound impact on your conversation without talking.

Avoiding touching your face

If you want to speak without words then do avoid your face while having a conversation. The idea of avoidance comes with time and you need to avoid other properly if you believe that you can make a strong impact on others life. Therefore, while you are able to have a strong impact of conversation try your best in making the lives of others way too better and you can do this while knowing how to avoid touching others' faces. Thus, the very way to make others avoid your face is by listening to the true alternates of your life and with the passage of time, you will have a strong impact on your conversation.

The morals of Public speaking

If you want to speak gently in front of the public then learn to speak to the inner thoughts of yourself. This means that you have to be very gentle and firm in your league and with the passage of time, you will understand how public speaking can be done more effectively. Therefore, the very idea of public speaking comes with time and in order to make the public a better place, you have to convey the idea in a much better and positive manner. Therefore, the morals of public speaking are everything that you need to know while you are speaking.

How body Language works

There is a strong saying that you cannot hide your lying eyes. The eyes of you are so intact while you are speaking and the body language that is used for this purpose is further augmented if you are able to have better results in the following. Body language works by making the eyes, the shoulders, the facial expressions and the saying tactics in a strong manner holistically. Therefore, body language comes with the passage of time and it works if you are smart in conversation, precise to the topic and relevant in the mode of comprehension. This is how the body language of the citizen properly.

Decoding Body Language

Body language can be decoded by using the following aspects of the conversation.

Facial Expressions

Body language can be easily assessed if one is able to recognize the facial expressions of others and while doing so. The facial expressions give a lot of consensus making while they are able to give solid expressions in the coming time. These facial expressions are a must to be used in the coming time and if one has to deploy strong expressions in his demand then all these things need to be employed pragmatically.

Body Proxemics

Body Proxemics is a way to up bring the closeness in a person and it is regarded as the best way to decode someone's body language. If you are new in the decoding business then you must harbor the use of body proxemics in your daily life. This concept will make the body straighten up in a close manner and with the passage of time, it will be uploaded in a frank manner. Therefore, body proxemics will let the decoding of the body language function in a better way.

Ornaments

If the person has worn some ornaments then the ornaments will help you understand the body language of that person in an effective manner. For instance, if there are some bands and chains on the human body then such ornaments depict the pluralist nature of the individual. Similarly, the makeup on the individual will set the human respect affect in a perpetual manner. Therefore, ornaments have a strong version of intellect in the person's body effectively.

Easily Read Body Language

This portion will deal with the argument about how language is properly instructed and easily read.

Study the eyes

If you are listening to somebody then carefully understand the body language of the individual. The eyes give you the strong reservation of the personality and with the passage of time, one is able to manifest strong feelings of the people in the coming time. Therefore, the eyes of the public are the reflection of the people and with the passage of time, you are able to induce strong commitments to the people.

Gaze at the face

You have to gaze at the face of the individual to know that if he is fine or not. This mode of interpretation will make you get a lot of respect in the facial expression. The gazing of the face is an important mode of understanding the person and with the passage of time, the person will get more understanding of the personality. Therefore, the gazing at the face is an important way to make things a little better and to decode the body language of a person effectively.

See if the person is mirroring you

The person, who is able to mirror you effectively will make the expression of the face in a pertinent manner. The person, who is mirroring you is able to read the minds and expressions of the person and with the passage of time, the person has many agitations in the coming time. The person that is able to induce mirroring in the person's mind will be able to give strong agitation in the coming time. Therefore, the person needs some of the socializing manners in it due to which it is able to induce frustration in the coming.

Observe the head movement

Observing the head movement will make you realize that the head of the person is something that will make the situation look more difficult and agitated in its construct. The observance of the head is as strong as it is perceived by the individual and with the passage of time, the person is able to give more and more agitation in the coming time. Therefore, the observance of the head movement is as crucial and cruel in its nature and that can lead to a strong mode of disturbance in the coming time.

Watch for the hand's signals

The person's hand signals are those signals that make the person look more agitative and frustrated in the coming time. The person can do a lot of socialization when he is able to do hand signals and use them reflectively in the coming. The shaking of the person's mind can lead to a strong agitation in the coming time and the watch can retain a lot for the individuals in the coming time. Therefore, the watch of the hand's signals can lead to strong construction in the coming time and this could be very effective in the coming time.

Examine the position of the arms

The position of the arms can be selected for the better nourishment of the people. If the person is able to do a better examination of the position of arms then he is able to read the body language of the person in an effective manner. The examination of the position of the arms can unfold many realizations of the person and the person is able to manifest the minds of others in a humble way. Therefore, the examination of the position of arms can reflect the body language of the person in an effective manner and in order to understand the person's mind, the man will able to reflect the nourishment of the women in a pertinent manner.

How to read your own body language

This portion of the chapter will look into the consideration of reading the language of the other personality.

Seeing the mirror and observing your acute expressions

If you want to observe the body language of yourself then see the expression of yourself in the mirror. With the passage of time, the person will give you a lot of concentration and you will come to know a lot of assertion in the coming time. You will come to realize that you have some other aspects of yourself and with the passage of time, you will decode your own body language. The crossed legs and the strong eye set depict that you are not in the mood of others to watch you. The seeing of the mirror and the observance of acute expression will provide a lot of assertions in the coming time.

Therefore, the more you look into the mirror, the more you are able to have a better understanding of yourself in the coming time.

Chapter 3 How to read people

Reading people is another way of making the people think about themselves and with the passage of time, the people admire such qualities. The contents of this chapter are as follows:

Considerations about reading people's mind

1. Isolation

Isolation starts with the basics of brainwashing. The brainwashing is important to understand by the manipulator. The manipulator would use the edifice of isolation. The isolation is effective in its use and by all means necessary, the manipulator tends to isolate you from the social order. He makes you understand that the world is not effective in its use and can be very haunting in its meaning. Therefore, isolation is a technique used to be understood effectively.

2. Attacks on self-esteem

While brainwashing, the manipulator uses the edifice of attacks on self-esteem. For him, the brain of you is of high importance. Whatever he thinks of you can be altered only if he wishes to change your brain. You will make the self-esteem of yourself and by the prospects you will understand that the manipulator is using this edifice to brainwash you.

3. Mental abuse

In order for the brainwashing to work more effectively, the use of mental abuse is of high importance. The use of mental abuse will work in a practical manner and will thwart the conformity of the brain precisely. The mental abuse can be used of mentality and effectively and with the passage of time, you will understand that you are seeking to feel very obscene. Therefore, the crux of mental abuse will be effective for you in its making.

4. Physical abuse

The physical abuse will look into the brainwashing in a complete manner. Do your best to avoid the physical abuse of the manipulators. Otherwise, you will find yourself in a turbulent manner. The physical abuse can lead to the tarnishing of the brain and you will feel very bad at the end. Therefore, the concept of physical abuse must never be allowed to be furnished in the first place.

5. Only allowing contact with selected members

Brainwashers or manipulators want you to contact with selected members. The selected members will cater to the brainwashing effectively and with the passage of time, they can be successful if you do not object them in the first place. The selected members will showcase a culture of degeneration among you and with the passage of time, you will feel very bad and bodacious. Therefore, the contact hearing is only important for you if you wish to understand the nature of the selected members.

6. Us versus them

This slogan will make you understand that the entire slogan of unity will forever haunt you. The brainwashing gets its momentum when it is trending at a larger scale and there is a policy of us contamination with them syndrome. This means that the US is not able to engage them processors and with the passage of time, the people are able to have a strong fan page about it.

7. Lie less and do more

The deceiving personality knows that he has to make sure of his conversations. If he lies more and more then he will get under the curve of badness and with the passage of time, he will feel himself to be bad. Also, there is a chance of him to get caught and could end himself in a bad manner.

Therefore, in deception, the manipulator lies less and less and gets away from it.

8. Telling the truth in a misleading manner

Telling the truth in a misleading manner means that one has to be very effective in its regard. The telling of truth in a misleading manner showcases the strength of personalities and hence, the people are able to be maneuvered in a better way. Therefore, the deceiving personality uses the edifice of deception to make sure that the individual is all bad and worse in the frame.

9. The deceiver knows his target

The deceiver always does his best in knowing the target in an effective manner and when he approaches in an acute way, he tends to be very effective and efficacious in its rating. Therefore, the use of deception is a tool to know the target effectively and the time taken for its progress will also be used in a longer way.

10. Keep your facts straight

The keeping of facts straight makes you understand what are the uses of fact measures. The idea is simply that the deceiving personality uses the facts straight and effective in its regard and with the passage of time, the facts are quite pertinent in its regard. Therefore, the keeping of facts means that the person is able to have a strong version of manipulation in him.

11. Staying Focused

The idea of staying focused is that the art of deception requires stealth and help. The stealth requires strong focus and assertion and with the passage of time, the man has to be very strong and sturdy in its manner. The focus paradigm will come in its manner and hence, the person is able to have a core function of its people.

12. Watch your signals

The people are able to have a strong set of affection for themselves. The idea is simply that the deceiving personality will focus on the coming signals and with the passage of time, the personality will do its best in making the game more astute and effective. Therefore, the idea is simple for the psychologist and the manipulator to handle.

13. Always turn up the pressure

Turning up the pressure will always make the people look more and more agile. The pressure comes with a stringent mode of affection and with the passage of time, the manipulator makes it look easier and more effective. Therefore, the use of pressure can ease the process in a curbing manner and thus, the deception will make the process more and more great.

Techniques to read easily people

1. Do all the thinking

The manipulators will do their best in doing the thinking for you. They will think for you and will tell you the best for you. However, doing revolves around the crux of manipulation. They are doing this so that you can be in their domain and thus, there mind control tactic is successful. This is the better prospect for you and once you do this, you are in the action of the mind control.

2. Starting an avalanche

The avalanche is a marketing firm that makes you strong and subtle in their regard. The creation of an avalanche is pertinent for you to understand and with the passage of time, there is secret maneuvering for you and you will induce an avalanche for you. The avalanche for you is that you have to be in the claws of an avalanche for you. Therefore, the mindset of the individual is easily dodging and with the passage of time, he is able to have control of the manipulator.

3. Ask for an inch take a mile

The asking for an inch and taking a mile is a concept that asserts the importance of taking things quickly. This means that the manipulator would cast a shadow quickly and with the passage of time, he would ask things for you which would have no actual reasons. This can be explained with an example. The manipulator would do a big favor for you and in return, you would love to comply with him and with the passage of time, the manipulator would not take your compliments. He would ask of something great and then he would take a profuse amount. This is the basic tenant of manipulation that asks something else and gets an all-in return.

4. Always have a real deadline

The real deadline means that the person has to realistically forecast a shadow line on you and you are not expected to do anything in return. The deadline means that you will do something for him and in return, he will give you proper isolation for you. Therefore, it is important to understand the nature of you and you will have the prospects in no time. The real deadline refers to the last concept of the material and with the passage of time, you will get a new result in the formation.

5. Giving ten times more

The manipulator will be able to leverage himself by giving you more and more things. If he does something for you and in return you do better for him. Then this is the mode of affection for him. Therefore, the giving of ten-time will provide you a sustainable moment of affection for yourself. This is exactly the method of utilization for you and you will be able to have more relaxation of it. Therefore, the giving of more things is actually a way to control the minds of the public and he will get more and more insight into it. Thus, the giving of more and more things will provide you with better affection.

6. Standing for something greater for you

The people are able to get in your mind control if they believe in you. In order for them to believe in you, you have to do something great for them. To an extent, that they will always recall of you while they are pursuing something and they are able to have a problem in any situation. In this way, they will harbor all the mechanisms for you that will induce a great sense of affection for you. Therefore, standing for something is actually an act of affection for you and the people around you.

7. Be shameless

The people are always shameless, who want to manipulate you carefully. They feel as it is their importance to have you onboard for their progression. They believe that people will understand you effectively if they are shameless. Being shameless does not mean that they dance in all nudity for you but in actual terms, they are able to have a strong sense of affection for you. Therefore, being shameless is an attribute to you so that you are able to have a precautionary sense of affection in you.

8. Eye seduction

In psychology, you can use the edifice of eye to eye connection in order to make the eyes look greater and more effective. The eye effect is important to seduce the other end of personalities. The personalities are able to have a great sense of seduction in them due to which the public is able to have fun and persuasion. The eye seduction is tantamount to give more and more value to the psychologists and in time, they are able to have more fun and zeal in eye seduction. Thus, it is important to do eye seduction in the coming time.

9. Using the lack nesses

In dark psychology, you can use the lack of nesses of other personalities so that you can have leverage on other personalities. You will understand in time that the individuals will be able to have more and more zeal in them. The lack of nesses can give you more aspects of their clout. The clout can be more incisive in their regard. The use of edifice can help you give more and more aspiration in the coming. The psychologist and the manipulator will use this prospect to gain leverage in the coming time.

Tricks for reading people's thoughts

1. He is charming and nice

The manipulator is all charm and nice at first. He would try his best in making you feel comfortable and gradually, he would impart his shrewdness. First, he would come in your comfort zone by wishing you birthdays, by giving you gifts and making you feel less agitated about anything then he would cast his dogmas. Once he knows that you will not bother him about anything then he would tell you to do anything by all means necessary. Sometimes, his manipulation is so strong and stringent that he can make you do anything even murder. Thus, this is the idea of manipulation that is started with charming voices and ending in catastrophe. Beware of such people.

2. Denial

The manipulator would always deny any assertion or statement of guilty on him. He would be felt exempt from any charges and would dare to see himself in the crux of any problem. If you somehow even manage to bring him in any disaster then he would just simply run away and would assert his innocence overcharges. He would think of himself as a strong mode of eccentricity and he would deny any kind of charges on him and would plead his innocence all over time. This is the true nature of denial that it tends to be very compulsive and bad in its progression and becomes haunting as well. Therefore, the denial is able to make the people look very bad and obsolete to the individual.

3. Lying

The people are able to lie a lot and those, who can actually conform themselves on it are lying. The lying edifice starts with the inculcation of hate speech and derogation and with the passage of time, the people tend to learn a lot of lying. The innocents are not able to see the manifestation of lying in their inner sides and they do not how exactly is the platform of lying quite degenerate about it. The lying helps the manipulator to learn more and more about the advances of the individual and with the passage of time, he comes one step closer tin dodging and abhorring you. This is the strong crux of lying that needs to be strengthened by all means necessary.

4. Excessive Flattery

This sign is of huge importance to the manipulator. The manipulator is able to do a lot of flattery for the individuals and with the passage of time, the individual can harbor flattery and sweetness among the individuals. The flattery helps to manipulate the individuals in a strong manner and this flattery can be of any side and sustenance. The idea exhibited here is quite strong as the people are able to create an environment of justice and order in the citizens and the flattery helps to regulate themselves in an effective manner.

5. Forced Teaming

The individual can use the teaming of the layers for his own motives. This teaming can be devious in its nature and can reflect many ills and whims of the societies. The teaming can also lead to social segregation in society and with the passage of time, the person can easily regulate its crux in a mature manner. The force teaming can appoint strong versions of impact for the students and with the passage of time, the individuals can come up with strong assertions. The forced teaming could be the use of any strength and value and it could be very destructive in its nature as well. Therefore, forced teaming is a sign of affection for the manipulator and it is destruction for the students as well.

6. Good First Impression

The manipulator will always do his best to make the best impression that he can in order to carefully influence the minds of other people. This is a well-managed task just to make sure that the audience is under the reflection of the manipulator and you will all mean necessary, follow under the trap of the manipulators. The good impression can be very expressive in its command and it can yield to proper potential as well but its lasting impacts are very pernicious. With the subtle use of a good impression, the person can easily establish his core links with you and can make you do almost everything. Therefore, a person having an expression of a good impression in him will be interpreted as a manipulator.

7. Pretending to be a victim

The manipulator is of a harsh and smart demeanor. He knows that if he pretends to be a victim then all the people will listen to him and no matter what are the conditions his stance and statements will stand correct. He will understand this assertion in a jiffy and will do his best to make the public very bad and obscene. The idea is simply that the person is not able to convey his true propositions to the public and he pretends to be a victim. The concept of victimhood tarnishes his image and with the passage of time, he tends to deviate from the straight path. This mere concept completely obstructs the use of empathy from the manipulator's mind and with the passage of time, he feels very degenerative. Therefore, the person, who is a manipulator, will always have a sign of victimhood in him.

8. Silent Treatment

This sign is of strong admiration in the person, who is playing to be a manipulator. The manipulator will easily treat the level of punishment to the audience and while doing this, he will be silent and stringent as hell. This is the idea of concealing and secrecy that the manipulator employees and with the passage of time, he is able to impart a devious mechanism of dealing with things upon the individual. Therefore, it is important to observe the silent treatment of things in the public and this silent treatment will actually make the person feel very atrocious. Therefore, in order to see the sign of manipulation the person has to be very silent and if he is found silent then yes, he is a manipulator.

9. Appearing to be selfless

The signs of selflessness are the signs that make the individual look very harsh and strong. The selflessness comes in the individuals either he has a golden heart or is he using the emblem of selflessness for himself. For instance, a boy, who is a manipulator falls in love with a person and asserts her to be selfless. At the moment, perhaps he is vouching for a love affair but in the true sense, he tends to be manipulative. He would cast the shadow of badness upon the girl just to have an advantage of her and even get something from her. Therefore, the use of selflessness is also a quality that needs to be strengthened properly.

10. Guilt Tripping

The idea of guilt-tripping is essential to understand as to decipher the nature of manipulation. In the guilt-tripping, the manipulator harbors the power of guilt in an individual and with the passage of time, he manipulates the other individual uses his guilt. He showcases that he is no the one, which is guilty and he trips the momentary aspects of guilt just to convey his innocence. This is a culture of guilt-tripping and it is easily found in all the corners of the world. Even international leaders use the edifice of guilt-tripping to transcend a culture of guilt-tripping. Therefore, it is important to understand that guilt-tripping can lead to a devastating blow of injuries and badness.

11. Shaming

When the manipulator easily acquires his motives, he starts shaming others. He feels that the individual is of no worth and in order to destroy him completely, he must be shamed. He would shame you using harsh means, he would kill you possibly, he would employ derogatory remarks upon you and he would instill a culture of deviance among you.

Therefore, the culture of shaming is found prevalent among the manipulators and if one has to recognize a manipulator, then he can use this edifice for good reasons. This is the revering identity of the individuals by all means necessary.

12. Intimidation

The person is able to intimidate the other personality if he is manipulative. The manipulation is a hectic task as it requires a lot of effort for the manipulator to intimidate you. This intimidation can be strong as it could lead to an effective mode of manipulation for the individuals. The intimidation starts with a turning point as it will create more efflux of opportunities for the personalities for you. This culture of intimidation is great as you can create more manipulative tactics for your self but in the end, it will be harsh for you. Therefore, it is mandatory to understand that intimidation is a recognizing aspect of a manipulator.

13. Diversion

Diversion refers to the diversity of opinion among the manipulators so that the people can easily lead to a better productive scenario of people to people contact. This diversity is important for you as it will yield a greater sense of affection for you and in the presence of time, you will be able to diversify your opinion based on a common strand of diversity. This means that the manipulator can use the edifice of diversity just to yield more manipulation and strength in him. This can be taken in the aspect of the plurality of opinion and in many ways, it can be dangerous as well.

Tips for reading people

The following are the ways of reading people.

Creation of a baseline

Creation of a baseline means that a person's identity is subjected. The baseline of the person is very good to interpret in the minds of the people and with the passage of time, the baseline is subjected to a powerful construct of happenings. These happenings will let to a better possibility of reading that person in a coherent manner and the creation of a baseline will help you understand the cognition of a person in a better way.

Look for deviations

Deviations mean that the person is not able to find strong connections of the person and the person is not able to create better complacency of the people in their lead. The look for deviation is an interim world, where the people are able to have strong connections in the coming. So, if you want to look in the world and see that the person is able to create some reflections in the past then see how he deviates in daily life. This is called the process of deviations, which imbue a process of agitation in the person for a longer run.

Compare and Contrast

You need to compare and contrast with the person with whom you want to be settled in the coming time. The comparison comes with the systematic evaluation of the process of the people and the people are able to have strong endurance about it. The contrasting factors come with respect to time and the people are able to create strong reservations about it. Therefore, the reservation that come through it will have comparison and contrast about it in the coming time.

Identify the strong voice

Identification of a strong voice is an important tool, which makes life easier with the process of socialization. The identification leads to the belief that the person having a strong voice will eventually create more tendencies in the coming. The strong voices will generate compassion in its life and with the passage of time, the people are able to store an identification of the socialized person. Therefore, the identification of a strong voice leads to a better way of understanding things effectively.

Pinpoint action words

Pinpointing action words means that you are able to have better decoding of the language in you with a better amount of time. The pinpointing of action means that the more you have a better reaction of the words, the more you have strong connections in it. The action words come with strong use of words and within time, you are able to have a better understanding of the person in the random list. So, do your best in pinpointing the action in people's lives if you want to make a better understanding of the people.

Look for personality clues

Try your best to make the best of the personality of yourself and try to look for more clues in the personality of others if you are willing to make new changes in the coming life. The personality clues come with a respected amount of time and you are able to induce better skeptics in the person for a longer duration of time. The look is a secret way for other personalities to understand the better way of indulging the rights of personalities in the coming time. Therefore, it is important to look for more options in a person and with the amount of coming time, the person is able to make better administration in the coming time. Thus, the possibility of clues is a better way to make things more pragmatic in the coming time and hence there is a lot of understanding, which can be helpful in the better running of time.

Gestures for interpreting people

They are many gestures through which many people can be interpreted. The following are some of the examples.

Standing with hands-on-hips

Standing with hands-on-hips is a strong assertive tone through which the person is able to have an impact of strength and quality. The person feels that the more he is acting like this, the more he is able to have better projections in life. The assertiveness comes with the time of strong critique and impact through which he is able to give out a bad manner in this regard. Standing with hands-on-hips is also a way of inducing strength and valor to the people.

Standing with legs crossed

Standing with legs crossed means that the person is able to induce submission and subtleness in the manner. The standing with legs crossed comes with the passage of time and the person is able to give a very submissive narrative in this regard. The standing with legs crossed is a reflection to a better mode of reflection to a person and this reflection helps to be sustained in a strong reflection of a person. Hence, standing with legs crossed is a hectic way of leading things in a better mode.

Standing with legs Uncrossed

Standing with legs uncrossed is a mode of reflection and collectiveness. The uncrossed legs marks optimism in a person and the person is able to induce better projections in the other person's mind. The mind of the person is so effective and leading that the person must contain strong emblems of optimism and co-relation in it. The standings come with a perpetual mode of affection in it and the person gives strong efforts of coordination to the person. Therefore, standing with legs uncrossed is a sign of better relief to a person and the person is able to deal with the person's mind collectively.

Touching or playing with hair

This is a sign that the person is not able to pay proper attention to another person holistically. The person, who is touching or playing with hair is a person that has a lot going on in his mind. He is a person with whom you want to have a strong chit chat about everything and you are able to induce a small set of capabilities in him. This person is very logical and effective in his brain and with the passage of time, he wants to deem better ways of understanding in the coming time.

The cowboy stance

This is a stance that is of a cowboy meaning. This means that you are not able to make better understandings of things and perhaps, the person is able to induce a better piece of understanding in the meantime. The cowboy stance is a stance that makes things look in a better way and there is a minor of complication that evolves around the concept of clarity in it. The cowboy stance is a stance that will help you look greater and more effective in the coming time. The stance is a strength of a person and the person is able to give the last impact of things in the coming time. The cowboy stance creates a better way of nourishment for a person and the person is able to have a strong impact on it in the coming time.

Covering the mouth

This is a person, who is very secretive in nature. He likes to talk about things as it is very bad in its construct. The constructs of the mouth are so great in its usage that the person can learn about skeptics and secrecy. Therefore, the covering of the mouth is a mouthpiece for secrecy and a person is able to commit a lot of ways to make sure that the person is about to induce clandestine nature in it. Thus, the use of covering the mouth is a better way to make things appear on the bright side.

Crossed Arms

It is an attitude that solidifies the crossing of a person in a perfect manner. The crossed arms gesture shows that the person is able to make the things go in a positive manner. The positive manner of a person is quite skeptical in this regard as well. The crossed arms help you to maintain better prospects in a person's mind and with the passage of time, the crossed arms will make a hefty price of installments in the coming time. Therefore, the crossed arms will give you a better way to understand things in a positive manner.

Chapter 4 How to detect lies

Lying is an obscene habit and it is used to detect the badness in a person and it should be made clear here that this book will look into the ways of detecting lies and bad qualities.

Chapter 4 How to Detect Lies

Verbal signs of Lying

A person who does the following things to you is actually lying and behaving in a belligerent manner.

1. Do all the thinking

The manipulators will do their best in doing the thinking for you. They will think for you and will tell you the best for you. However, doing revolves around the crux of manipulation. They are doing this so that you can be in their domain and thus, there mind control tactic is successful. This is the better prospect for you and once you do this, you are in the action of the mind control.

2. Starting an avalanche

The avalanche is a marketing firm that makes you strong and subtle in their regard. The creation of an avalanche is pertinent for you to understand and with the passage of time, there is secret maneuvering for you and you will induce an avalanche for you. The avalanche for you is that you have to be in the claws of an avalanche for you. Therefore, the mindset of the individual is easily dodging and with the passage of time, he is able to have control of the manipulator.

3. Ask for an inch take a mile

The asking for an inch and taking a mile is a concept that asserts the importance of taking things quickly. This means that the manipulator would cast a shadow quickly and with the passage of time, he would ask things for you which would have no actual reasons. This can be explained with an example. The manipulator would do a big favor for you and in return, you would love to comply with him and with the passage of time, the manipulator would not take your compliments. He would ask of something great and then he would take a profuse amount. This is the basic tenant of manipulation that asks something else and gets an all-in return.

4. Always have a real deadline

The real deadline means that the person has to realistically forecast a shadow line on you and you are not expected to do anything in return. The deadline means that you will do something for him and in return, he will give you proper isolation for you. Therefore, it is important to understand the nature of you and you will have the prospects in no time. The real deadline refers to the last concept of the material and with the passage of time, you will get a new result in the formation.

5. Giving ten times more

The manipulator will be able to leverage himself by giving you more and more things. If he does something for you and in return you do better for him. Then this is the mode of affection for him. Therefore, the giving of ten-time will provide you a sustainable moment of affection for yourself. This is exactly the method of utilization for you and you will be able to have more relaxation of it. Therefore, the giving of more things is actually a way to control the minds of the public and he will get more and more insight into it. Thus, the giving of more and more things will provide you with better affection.

6. Standing for something greater for you

The people are able to get in your mind control if they believe in you. In order for them to believe in you, you have to do something great for them. To an extent, that they will always recall of you while they are pursuing something and they are able to have a problem in any situation. In this way, they will harbor all the mechanisms for you that will induce a great sense of affection for you. Therefore, standing for something is actually an act of affection for you and the people around you.

7. Be shameless

The people are always shameless, who want to manipulate you carefully. They feel as it is their importance to have you onboard for their progression. They believe that people will understand you effectively if they are shameless. Being shameless does not mean that they dance in all nudity for you but in actual terms, they are able to have a strong sense of affection for you. Therefore, being shameless is an attribute to you so that you are able to have a precautionary sense of affection in you.

Tips for detecting lies in verbal discussion

You must have the following tactics in you to detect lies in any particular verbal discussion.

1. Repression

Repression means that you are about to forget the evil thoughts and mechanisms that could trigger agitation in you. You have to induce the spirit of repression in you so that you may able to forget all the bad thoughts and ideas that one has induced in you. You have to use the concept of acceptance and individualistic effort on you and therefore, you are able to have a stronger version of acceptance in you. Thus, repression acts as a strong defense mechanism and you are able to give viable justifications to it.

2. Projection

In this kind of a mental defense system, you have to project the positive feelings of any problem in front of you. You have to make sure that any negativity that comes into your mind is easily removed and you are able to have a solid grip on your comfortability of the thoughts. You need to make sure that any such ingredients that tend to distort your inner feelings are not hampered and are not projected in your mind. Therefore, the very idea of projecting good feelings in situations of bad feelings is named as projection. Thus, you need to govern these instruments effectively in the manner.

3. Displacement

Displacement means that you need to empower the inner thoughts of yourself in an effective manner and by any yardstick, you need to be pragmatic in the developments. The displacement helps you to engage others in a positive manner and you are able to have a sound impression of yourself. However, if you are not able to make a strong displacement of yourself then you are in the impression of the bad ones. Therefore, displacement helps you make the assertions come in an effective manner.

4. Rationalization

The rationalization mechanism works with the implementation of this principle that you need to come up with strong emotions in your brain. You can avoid any negativity in the atmosphere and most importantly, you cannot sustain without them either. You have to bolster rationalization in yourself so that you are able to have a sustainable feature of intellect in you. You need certain primaries in yourself while you are rationalizing. You have to be bold and independent in your saying and never let lose in front of others no matter what happens. Therefore, rationalization is a strong defense system that makes you believe in your self and no matter where you go, you are able to have a strong system of catering emotions through it.

5. Reaction Formation

The reaction formation is a concept, which indicates that once the negativity has been uttered upon you, you are able to form a reaction on it. The reaction is that you do not need to have a strong reservation about it but you must have the credibility of conjunction in you. The easiest way for you to form a reaction formation is that you need to believe in the formation of strong reactions. You can do them anytime in the coming time and you do not have to feel submerged while doing so. Therefore, the formation of reaction creation is another way to make way for strong opponents coming in the time.

6. Denial

In order to make the emotional mechanism of yourself up to date, you need to deny any such restrictions upon you and must do your best in denying any sort of imposition upon your character. For instance, if someone is imposing any alleged mark on you then you have to make the substance of the world in a reactive manner and must not upbring the concepts of the loser in a bad way. Thus, the denying process is the process that cultivates emotional uprising in you and in order to make, the world a better place, you need to deny any such impositions on you.

Tips for detecting lies in body language

There are six ways of detecting a liar in an acute manner.

Always ask neutral questions

Neutral questions mean that the person is able to ask many neutral questions that tend to derail the motion of the public in an acute manner. The people, who are able to mark black tendencies in public can do it very well. The process is very easy as it involves the powerful use of neutral skepticism and the person is able to have a better mode of understanding in the clear matter. The asking of neutral questions will ultimately lead you to the wrong place and you will come up with hectic assertions in a coming manner. Therefore, asking neutral questions will ultimately lead to the detection of lies.

Find the hot spot

The idea of a hot spot means that there is always a bad ending of a conversation through which a person is able to make bad impressions in the coming time. The hot spot is sometimes a bad way to make things go in a wrong manner. The hot spot of the construction comes with time and the person is able to do bad ways of engulfing things in a wrong manner. The hot spot is a way through which a person gets a lot of understanding in him and hence with the perpetual manner of finding the hot spot, he is able to do things wrong and obscene.

Watch Body language

If you want to detect the scheme of body language then ultimately you will come to this conclusion that how body language will make things work in an effective manner. The body language is a concept, which needs to be carefully understood with a person and with the passage of time, body language tends to deviate with the prospects of time. Therefore, body language is a sort of mode of conviction where one is able to have better understandings of others. Therefore, body language is a careful token which needs to be understood properly in order to have a better formation of lie detection.

Observe micro-facial expressions

The micro facial expression means that you are able to have a strong mode of lie detection in you and you are able to contain a strong sense of affection in you. The use of micro-facial expression will clearly lead you to a better manner and with the passage of time, you will understand how things unfold in a better yet sustainable option. Therefore, the use of micro facial expressions is a concept, which helps you to contain a strong facial mode of expression within you. Thus, the overall use of body language will make the individual affect the rate of things goes in a better way.

Listen to tone, cadence and structure

The listening to tone, cadence and structure is a way through which the person is able to detect lies in an effective manner. Whenever there is a discussion coming in the time, try your best to carefully observing the structure of language if you are able to have it. Understand that you are able to lead the psyche of the individuals carefully with the advent of time and thus, this is a better way of understanding things in a holistic manner. This is a way of making things float so that the person is able to have a better mode of aspiration in the longer run. So, cadence and structure can help things go in a positive manner.

Tips for detecting lies with intuition

Try to use the following gestures in order to form the detection in lied within an intuition.

1. Gaslighting

This is the technique that is used to see if the person's words sound like his actions or not. The gaslighting is a method that can be used to question the belief of the personality and with the passage of time, the person has to understand the use of this tool to use the manipulation effectively. There is a set of questions among the public, used by the manipulator to dodge the essence of the questions and with the passage of time, the entire scenario of the public changes with time all because of the gas questions, asked by the manipulator.

2. Generalizations

The generalizations of a manipulator are a strong sense of demotivation for the public to withstand. The manipulator easily generalizes all the terms and tactics that are employed on a social, economic and political factor and with the passage of time, the generalizations come with time. The generalizations are important enough for a manipulator for the student to understand the essence of all compatible reasons for the public and with the passage of time, the manipulator is able to see the distance of the public go far away. Therefore, the distance of the public from the real cause actually defines the status of the manipulator and the manipulator can control a lot of sense through it. Therefore, the use of a generalizing matter creates more and more aspect for the students and civilians. Thus, the use of generalization gives impetus to the manipulator and with the passage of time, it can be more asserted in the coming. So, generalization can lead to a lot of trouble and menace for the student.

3. Moving the goal post

The manipulators have every right to deny your goal and ambition. They call it the moving of goal post and this is how the public is able to induce bad and obscene mechanisms to it. The goal post is the ambition of every man to cater to the fundamentally obsessed question of the incident and with the passage of time, the manipulator tends to de-track you from the quest at the earliest. The track is therefore a sense of motivation for you and you do not get enough style of aspiration for the students and civilians. The idea is quite simple that the public is able to create more satisfaction for the public and with the passage of time, the manipulators induce havoc as well.

4. Changing the subject

The manipulator would do his best to change the subject. This aspect makes avoid accountability of his previous actions and with the passage of time, he learns the act of treachery and deception. Any time or anyplace, where he is not able to see the masterpiece of the subject, he tends to foil with the public and therefore, he is not even governing the matter of the public so that he could not even to the matter of appreciation.

Thus, changing the subject of any conversation is also a tool of manipulation that is required by all means necessary.

5. Name-calling

Name-calling is an art and tactic that can be used to induce marginalization in the incident and with the passage of time, it could lead to dilemmas and destruction. The name-calling starts with a mode of aspiration for the pupils but ends in utter destruction for the public. This concept can be easily seen in many areas and portions of the world and such a practice can induce horror and terror in the region. This practice of name-calling can be used in the factors that enable one with destruction and devastation.

6. Smear Campaigns

This campaign is used to address the horrendous use of psychology for the public. This is a play in which you are the victim and they are the martyr. According to them, you have displayed a sense of bad relationship to them and for that mere reason they have labeled you as a dead person. You no longer have a sense of reputation in the system and every time you encounter them, they tend to call you bad and the gone one. This aspect has many difficulties for you and ends up being a psychopath. This aspect has emotional issues for you, psychological issues for you, ovulational and many more. Therefore, smear campaigns are personally made to make you feel bad and obscene and with the passage of time, you feel very hectic.

7. Devaluation

This devaluation is not the currency devaluation but it is the human devaluation of yourself, you tend to be very bad and obsolete in your character that you embarrass every one's exes. You will as it is your pertinent duty to make the lives and ages of others feel embarrassing and with the passage of time, you control over your anger just to inflict punishment among the others. For instance, there was a time when people were able to cooperate with one another and could not try to defame others. However, with the burgeoning social media, people tend to decide the relationship of others by making them feel very degenerate. This is the crucial aspect of psychology, which could be very tumultuous for you and with the passage of time, he felt very bad and worse. Therefore, devaluation is meant to be an outlet of Body Language and it can be very harmful to anyone, who does it.

8. Aggressive Jokes

Aggressive Jokes are the modes to make others look small and in shambles. These jokes could be of anything like the jokes on individuality, the jokes on society and the jokes on caste. These jokes impose derogatory remarks on the individuals and with the passage of time, the individuals feel very bad about them. The idea is simply that psychology believes that manipulators could be the worst nightmares for innocent personalities. People can use the edifice of others to personally sabotage the concept of friendliness and equality among the people and with the passage of time, the people tend to showcase a system of defamation among others. Thus, aggressive jokes can be bad and hazardous to others.

9. Triangulation

This is the concept, in which the individuals tend to use the supposed threat of others to manipulate the innocents. Suppose there are three individuals in a room, two of them are having an argument about anything and the person sitting next to them is of a high caste. The manipulator would use the edifice of the supposed threat of the third person to deter that of a second person and with the passage of time, the concept of triangulation would be bolstered. Hence, the use of force and manipulation is done in order to make the third parties very bad and degenerate.

10. Use of tools

In this paragraph, the tools that can be used for manipulation will be discussed. These are sensory devices, visual sensors, automatic assembly, industrial manipulator and photoelectric detectors. These tools cast a shadow of degeneration among the personalities and with the passage of time, the people are able to have a list of traumata embedded in them. Therefore, with the passage of time the tools can be used for a stringent version of the collaboration.

Chapter 5 How to Analyze People

The final chapter will look into the thesis of how people are analyzed. The important contents of this chapter are as follows:

Secrets of Body Language

1. Body Language is universal in its nature

This claim asserts that Body Language is universal and needs to be implemented at a bigger level. No human being is immune to the dark conduct of life and he has to inflict pain on others just to exhibit a source of retaliation for the other individuals. Initially, he tends to be vindictive. However, with the process of time, he becomes more lenient and effective. But one thing cannot be ignored that Body Language is prevalent in modern and post-modern times and with the evolutionary crux of time, the human tends to be sadistic in its actions and gestures.

2. Body Languages the study of the human condition

Body Language is the study of the human condition and the condition does not necessarily have to be normal. The condition can be haunting and can be very managerial in its constructs as well. However, one thing needs to be understood carefully that the human condition has to be averse and adamant to evilness. This means that while studying dark psychology, one has to keep in mind that Body Language will inculcate a bad and worse human condition in them with the passage of time.

3. Body Language is replete of destructive behaviors

The Body Language has a concept of destruction that makes the human go beyond the character of positivity and purity. The individual is not able to have a stable concept of calmness and acceptability in it and have to be more lenient in order to understand the edifice of love. The individual faces some deep shrouds of destruction in him and this is the most devastating feature of Body Language in him. Therefore, this tenet needs to be comprehensively manifested for the proper extermination of bad feelings in an individual.

4. Body Language plants out a range of inhumanity

The Body Languages manifested in terms of inhumanity. The people that do inhuman acts are bound to construct in the name of dark psychology. The Body Language tells that people are the apex predators of the human nature and they can only evolve in the making, if they tend to be more delinquent in their constructs. This means that only that person can survive, who has the ability to rise against the odds and wants to be more compelling in its nature. Therefore, the term Body Language can also be described in the mode of inhumanity.

5. All people can be violent

The other tenet of Body language that every human, who breathes and has a predilection for doing anything will tend to be violent. This is the inherent quality of any individual and regardless of his and her intention, the individual needs to ascribe with the violent tendencies. Therefore, this tenet advocates that all people have to be very mature and strong when it comes to the acceptance of violent tendencies.

6. Body Language needs to be properly learned

This tenet of Body Language advocates that in order to know the harms and ills of dark psychology, one has to be incognizant of its progression. Body Language can start its journey as an effective wave of catastrophe and if not tackled with proper care then it can be very harmful to the people as well. In order to make a staggering impact on the halt of dark psychology, one has to eliminate any such mental or emotional prognosis that can lead to the emanation of darkness in oneself.

More in-depth techniques of reading people

1. Foot in the door

The foot in the door means that you are asking for a small favor first and then you ask for a dark favor. This is the favor that could be very effective for you and in term can lead to a bad and obscene prospect. The manipulator would first use the aspect of manipulation so that the people would listen to the manipulator and then the manipulator would charge his nutshells among the people. This is a devious terminology, which is designed to give more and more agitation to the public.

2. Door in the face

For this technique to b effectively implemented, it is important for the manipulator to ask something, which is quite easy and effective for you. The door in the face means that you ask for something very subtle and you tend to be affectionate in its manner. The asking is polite and it is something, which is easily accessible by the people, but with the passage of time, the offer gets more invitation and you tend to disagree with it. Therefore, this offer is a gateway for the manipulator to have his ends meet.

3. Anchoring

Anchoring helps you to give leverage on many problems and the manipulator can easily use it to display a sense of affection for the public. The affection starts with an offer and then the manipulator fulfills to price required to do the job. This pricing is a gateway for the personalities to understand the essence of anchoring and the people, get to know the essence of manipulation in an easier manner. This anchoring can also be interpreted as pricing and once the manipulator fulfills the ideologies of anchoring then the person gets the idea in an effective manner.

4. Commitment and Consistency

The commitment and consistency are a gateway for the manipulator to get to know the advancements of issues and with the passage of time, he also fulfills them. The commitment and consistency are necessary for the manipulator to the harbor and with the passage of time, the people are able to distill the level of trust with the manipulator. The manipulation is an important mode of affection for the people and thus, with the passage of time, the manipulator gets to know the advancements in a better manner.

5. Social Proof

This is a smart persuading technique, in which the person uses the social proof and it maintains a link of affection for the other people. The manipulator easily creates a sense of ideological confrontation for the people and the people can get a large sense of commitment through it. This means that there is a disembarking of an idea that is followed by all and by strong assertion, the person is able to have a strong moment of content for the people. Therefore, with the passage of time, the person is able to have strong social proof in the coming time.

6. Authority

For persuading anyone, it is vital that the manipulator holds authority in his hand. The use of force and the compelling nature of the manipulator will serve his interest in a better manner and together, the manipulator is able to cast a great shadow of maneuvering among the people. Thus, the authority rests in the house of officials and the manipulator and this technique can be used in many of the forms efficiently. Authority commands dignity.

7. Scarcity of Resources

Manipulators try to market their assertions in a common manner. They will show as something is unavailable in the market and will showcase its assertions in a common manner. With the passage of time, the scarcity is carefully ensured by the marketer of the individual and he is not able to formulate better postures of it. He shows as if he has the authority of all the commands but the scarcity of the resources is a way to dodge the loyalty of other personalities. Therefore, the scarcity of resources is a method to employ good means of manipulation for the students and the pupils as well. Therefore, it is essential to understand the nature of manipulation and regardless of any issues, the scarcity is an endeavor to boost manipulation among the manipulator.

8. Reciprocation

Reciprocation is a method to persuade as well. When times the individuals are able to harbor the context of reciprocation, they channel the crux of reciprocation. Many times, the individuals are not able to reciprocate the concept of affiliation and they want to unnecessarily reciprocate. This reciprocation is done to show how the people are able to transform their lives and they have the pertinence of other individuals as well. Many times, the individual has done something for the public and the public does not want any reciprocation but still there is reciprocation.

These were the techniques of dark persuasion and now the techniques of mind control will be

Case Studies and Proper Examples

1. Freud's interest in Young Woman

This was the experiment that was conducted on the behest of Freud's relations with young women. In his Dark continuum, Freud believed that women, who do excessive masturbation are designed to be bad in nature and this is an ill-coordinated exercise that needs to be stopped. His experiments were many young women and out of them, was a young lady named, Emma. Emma had problems with anxiety and depression and she used to do a lot of masturbation just to make the pain go away and ace the mental trauma. She decided that she will never ever dare to pursue a relationship and in order to ace herself, she went for a doctor, who happened to be Freud. Freud made her inhale serious nostril drugs, which made her go dizzy and how was she treated, remained a mystery for long. The concept of Mind of the dark can be seen in these experiments, where Freud is testing the enduring skills of Emma and wants to carry on the experiment at the cost of every result. The mind control process is clearly exhibited in this experiment and such kind of tendencies are easily put forward in the mind of other people.

2. Electroshock Therapy on Children

Dr. Lauretta Bender of the Creedmoor Hospital believed that children, who do not have any social order in their characters are prone to be tested under an electroshock machine. She would invite many students to her lab and would not see the problems of the children clearly rather would ask some tough questions that would draw children towards the confusion. When the children aren't able to answer it then she would put them under an electroshock computer and with the passage of time, the children would lose their subconsciousness and be paranoid. This aspect, according to Dr. Lauretta was a tool to make the children active and strong but, in its progression, the experiments proved their worth. Instead, piles of bodies of dead children became the terrible outcome of such results. This is the kind of therapy, where the person is able to have a strong version of its concepts practically and it can be put under the ambit of mind control effectively. The use of mind control can take the people to strong limelight and with the passage of time, there are many assertions and comprehensions in it.

3. Operation Midnight Climax

The CIA, in the mid-sixties, wanted to study the concept and outcomes of LSD on students and civilians. The idea was that the agency wanted a leveraging study on drug trafficking, sex trafficking and the conduct of sexual abuses in the city of Los Angeles and Washington. The agency would hire female prostitutes and they would send it would send the females to the rooms of drug lords. The prostitutes would contaminate the situations for the lords and gradually, compel them to spill the beans for drug trafficking. Here, Mind Control was passing with the concept of Controlling the Factor of Mind , where the agency, on the behest of its authority, wanted to have a command on the drug lords. Mind control of mind and personality is clearly put forward in this experiment, where people are able to have a strong version of a personality framework of it. The use of operation can lead to a strong process of cultivation in it and hence, with the passage of time, the midnight climax would lead to proper assertions in the person.

4. The Monster Study

This study was carried out by Dr. Wendell Johnson and Mary Tudor and they studied twenty-two children with imperfect care and zeal. They brought the children to their houses and created two groups of children. One group was given positive speech notes and they were praised for their slight bit of contribution while speaking. The other group was a negative speech note, where every word of the child, was belittled and defamed. The outcomes of this study were dark as well, because the children's mental cognition and behavioral practices never became as per the requirements of a sane individual and the research became very petrified about this. This Monster Study was never really published because of the fear that the researchers might get arrested for it. The mind control was the main pillar of this study and the people wanted to make good assertions in this regard to the public. This was done to make the process look all good and pale. Therefore, mind control is implemented in this experiment effectively.

5. Project MKUltra

From the year 1953 to 1973, the United States conducted a series of manipulating experiments for their citizens. The reason for such experiments was to induce, excessive drug use, the use of harsh words, emotional abuse, sexual abuse, psychological abuse and whatnot. The results became very hedonistic in their nature and ultimately the cases and subjects were meant to be shut down. The project MKUltra was halted by Congress and in time, it was politically removed for the betterment of society.

6. The Aversion Project

This historical dark process was a landmark in the Dark continuum. The apartheid era in South Africa was on its horizon and many people had to be displaced from their homelands seeking refugee in neighboring countries. The spree of homosexuality was prevalent in South Africa and they wanted to cure themselves in a therapist manner. Dr. Aubrey Levin was put in charge by the government of the USA to cure the plight of homosexuals. According to the doctor back then, the people of homosexuals were facing a mental disorder due to which, homosexuals were unable to cure themselves. They started fleeing themselves away and the doctor wanted to erase their sexual orientation by making them realize the harms of being a homosexual. The idea was that the homos must be displaced with nude pictures of gays and lesbians and they will be forced to curse them. Doing this, will make them unable to have any kind of love affiliation with any gay and they will feel all great and strong. Therefore, the aversion project was done on the sole purpose of how gays and lesbians are evil and bad in their utter character and quite possibly, this project can lead to success and sustenance. The use of Mind control is another demeanor of the humans and with the passage of time, there are many experimentations in the public through which the public is able to have a sound mode of mind control. The mind control is an experiment that can be used to make the humans and other frameworks look greater and assertion.

7. Unnecessary Sexual Reassignment

This process is a heinous work of mind control. In this experiment, the mind control of the public is directly controlled and the person is able to have a lasting impact on the people effectively. The effect of such a gesture will create more tendencies in the mind of the public and with the passage of time, the person has to be very cordial in its structure. Sexual Reassignment is a process, which tends to reassign and alter the sex of an individual through biological and scientific means. This process came to limelight when a nine-year-old boy's gender was reassigned as doctors were not sure of his apparent gender. His penis was circumcised during a mental process and with the passage of time, he had to be reassigned further. This trauma was a severe condition for the parents and they did not know what measures they need to adopt to finish this problem. They want to the doctors bashing their claims and the people had to face some observations regarding this matter as well. Therefore, this was a dark process, which was made to induce a horror spirit in the children of people so that they could remain isolation in their approach.

8. Stanford Prison Experiment

The idea is simple in its research. The research comes with time and longevity and this is This experiment was conducted in the midst of 1971, where prisoners and guard men were able to speak to one another and the people had to face the moral outcome of it. It is important to understand that the mind-controlling phenomenon of the prisoners and it is used to make the public go efficient about the mind game of the people. The idea was there needing to be the depiction of the cause between prisoners and guards and then their culture of interaction could be studied better. The people, who had been given the role of the guard were taking their respective genres in a bad manner. The prisoners began to enforce harsh measures on the guards and the guards were not able to confess the suitability of that as well. The prisoners accepted the abuses in a rational manner and the people had to flee away from the cause by all means necessary.

9. Milgram Experiment

Mind control was used to be done in order to make the conduct of the person more reliable and efficient in its making. This experiment was used to see the level of assessment of the public and with the process of time, it created more realms of study. This experiment was conducted to understand the nature of the Nazis, after world war two. This Milgram experiment was designed to see if the patient is able to see the harsh realities of life and can be conformed to the authority or not. There was a test tube that was placed on the sides of the patient and a questioning panel was placed in front of him. The panel asked some nefarious questions to him and made him realize that he was quite incompetent and could not able to answer good and subtle answers. This proved a dark mechanism in the minds of the people and the panel that psychology is very relevant in the scenario of people. Therefore, the Milgram experiment was a torturing way to express sorrow and sadness in the minds of people and hence, it was expunged off or halted by the people by all means necessary.

10. The Monkey Drug Trials

This event was an epitome of Mind Control in which animals were tested. They were injected with drugs and the outcomes of drugs were carefully examined by the public. The public rendered its advice to the people and made sure that how the reaction would lead the animals. This reaction was a necessary ingredient of the testing of animals and it was asserted in the means of people by all means necessary. The monkey trial gave a dark side of psychology to the public and with the passage of time, it was assured that monkeys are a detriment to society. Therefore, the monkey drug trials exhibited a darker version of the animals as well and people came to this result very quickly.

11. Facial Expressions Experiment

This experiment was conducted on the basis of studying the facial expression of people while providing them an external stimulus. In this experiment, it was asserted that people that have some mental troubling issues would be given an external stimulus so that the people are able to have an impact on it. The facial expressions are there to judge the internal conditions of the individuals and then the personalities of the individuals are carefully assessed. The system is quite inherent in this manner and the people are able to give proper justification to the external responses. The external responses include the use of drugs, porn movies, the inducing of drugs and devastation and many more. The facial expression experiment gives the students and the clients a justification that the people are not able to have a sustainable presence in them.

12. Little Albert

This was the dark hour of the psychological era. The founder of behaviorism, Mr. John Watson was deemed as the dark executor of this regime and he named some of the children to be equally liable in this regard. He would take a young child in his custody and he would test the abilities of him. Little baby Albert was exposed to many sounds and another stimulus, which made him feel quite bad and slurry. This was done to condition fear of little Albert and with the passage of time, Albert was made quite inhumane in this regard. Therefore, little Albert had to be taught something great about the channeling of darkness and atrocity in the present and with the passage of time, Mind Control made this landmark achievement that psychology can also be used to condition fear and badness.

Chapter 6 Types of mind control

Following are the three common type of Mind Control

Other modes of Mind Control

There are many other modes of Mind Control that need to be described as well in order to get a close look at the dark methods of psychology.

1. Dark Mindset

The Dark Mindset is a set of imaginary lines and circles through which the public is able to get a dark side of almost everything. These circles are based on thoughts, feelings and perceptions that can lead to the task of sadistic ion by a dark body. Once you are in this circle of violence, you are not able to feel purposeful or have any sort of ambition and aim in you. The psychological maneuvering of Mind Control can lead to the mental past of illusion and fragmentation that can be horrendous in their making.

2. Controlling the Factor of Mind

Controlling the Factor of Mind is an apparent real of possibilities and potentials that are provident in all forms of humans. Controlling the Factor of Mind will make you feel terrible at times when you are morally or socially dysfunctional. The Controlling the Factor of Mind can even welcome a spree of negativity upon you due to which you will feel ashamed and be in shambles. Controlling the Factor of Mind can cause a lot of tension and agitation for you as well. Therefore, Controlling the Factor of Mind is a dark emblem, which is stored in us and could lead all of us to horror and terror.

3. The mind of the dark

The Mind of the dark is a concept that will be related and comprehended in terms of

Astro-physics and astrology. The singularity is a small and dense particle of the dark hole, which is present in the center of the hole and it has a minimum space of energy in it. The Mind of the dark believes that people, who are inflicted by it are bound to suffer from the horrors of isolation and estrangement. There are at par with every condition of life and there is a considerable amount of distance in between them and the space that is coming to them.

Chapter 7   Mind control techniques

1. Gaslighting

This is the technique that is used to see if the person's words sound like his actions or not. The gaslighting is a method that can be used to question the belief of the personality and with the passage of time, the person has to understand the use of this tool to use the manipulation effectively. There is a set of questions among the public, used by the manipulator to dodge the essence of the questions and with the passage of time, the entire scenario of the public changes with time all because of the gas questions, asked by the manipulator.

2. Generalizations

The generalizations of a manipulator are a strong sense of demotivation for the public to withstand. The manipulator easily generalizes all the terms and tactics that are employed on a social, economic and political factor and with the passage of time, the generalizations come with time. The generalizations are important enough for a manipulator for the student to understand the essence of all compatible reasons for the public and with the passage of time, the manipulator is able to see the distance of the public go far away. Therefore, the distance of the public from the real cause actually defines the status of the manipulator and the manipulator can control a lot of sense through it. Therefore, the use of a generalizing matter creates more and more aspect for the students and civilians. Thus, the use of generalization gives impetus to the manipulator and with the passage of time, it can be more asserted in the coming. So, generalization can lead to a lot of trouble and menace for the student.

3. Moving the goal post

The manipulators have every right to deny your goal and ambition. They call it the moving of goal post and this is how the public is able to induce bad and obscene mechanisms to it. The goal post is the ambition of every man to cater to the fundamentally obsessed question of the incident and with the passage of time, the manipulator tends to de-track you from the quest at the earliest. The track is therefore a sense of motivation for you and you do not get enough style of aspiration for the students and civilians. The idea is quite simple that the public is able to create more satisfaction for the public and with the passage of time, the manipulators induce havoc as well.

4. Changing the subject

The manipulator would do his best to change the subject. This aspect makes avoid accountability of his previous actions and with the passage of time, he learns the act of treachery and deception. Any time or anyplace, where he is not able to see the masterpiece of the subject, he tends to foil with the public and therefore, he is not even governing the matter of the public so that he could not even to the matter of appreciation. Thus, changing the subject of any conversation is also a tool of manipulation that is required by all means necessary.

5. Name-calling

Name-calling is an art and tactic that can be used to induce marginalization in the incident and with the passage of time, it could lead to dilemmas and destruction. The name-calling starts with a mode of aspiration for the pupils but ends in utter destruction for the public. This concept can be easily seen in many areas and portions of the world and such a practice can induce horror and terror in the region. This practice of name-calling can be used in the factors that enable one with destruction and devastation.

6. Smear Campaigns

This campaign is used to address the horrendous use of psychology for the public.

This is a play in which you are the victim and they are the martyr. According to them, you have displayed a sense of bad relationship to them and for that mere reason they have labeled you as a dead person. You no longer have a sense of reputation in the system and every time you encounter them, they tend to call you bad and the gone one. This aspect has many difficulties for you and ends up being a psychopath. This aspect has emotional issues for you, psychological issues for you, ovulational and many more. Therefore, smear campaigns are personally made to make you feel bad and obscene and with the passage of time, you feel very hectic.

7. Devaluation

This devaluation is not the currency devaluation but it is the human devaluation of yourself, you tend to be very bad and obsolete in your character that you embarrass every one's exes. You will as it is your pertinent duty to make the lives and ages of others feel embarrassing and with the passage of time, you control over your anger just to inflict punishment among the others. For instance, there was a time when people were able to cooperate with one another and could not try to defame others. However, with the burgeoning social media, people tend to decide the relationship of others by making them feel very degenerate. This is the crucial aspect of psychology, which could be very tumultuous for you and with the passage of time, he felt very bad and worse. Therefore, devaluation is meant to be an outlet of Mind Control and it can be very harmful to anyone, who does it.

8. Aggressive Jokes

Aggressive Jokes are the modes to make others look small and in shambles. These jokes could be of anything like the jokes on individuality, the jokes on society and the jokes on caste. These jokes impose derogatory remarks on the individuals and with the passage of time, the individuals feel very bad about them. The idea is simply that psychology believes that manipulators could be the worst nightmares for innocent personalities. People can use the edifice of others to personally sabotage the concept of friendliness and equality among the people and with the passage of time, the people tend to showcase a system of defamation among others. Thus, aggressive jokes can be bad and hazardous to others.

9. Triangulation

This is the concept, in which the individuals tend to use the supposed threat of others to manipulate the innocents. Suppose there are three individuals in a room, two of them are having an argument about anything and the person sitting next to them is of a high caste. The manipulator would use the edifice of the supposed threat of the third person to deter that of a second person and with the passage of time, the concept of triangulation would be bolstered. Hence, the use of force and manipulation is done in order to make the third parties very bad and degenerate.

10. Use of tools

In this paragraph, the tools that can be used for manipulation will be discussed. These are sensory devices, visual sensors, automatic assembly, industrial manipulator and photoelectric detectors. These tools cast a shadow of degeneration among the personalities and with the passage of time, the people are able to have a list of traumata embedded in them. Therefore, with the passage of time the tools can be used for a stringent version of the collaboration.

Thus, these are some of the ways and tools of manipulation that can harbor bad deeds in the person.

Chapter 8 Use of neuro-linguistic programming to improve self-esteem, manage one's feelings and believe in oneself

Neuro-Linguistic Programming

The use of neuro-linguistic programming is a method, which is used to cater to depression and anxiety. On an international level, the use of NLP is done in order to make the programming look more easier and effective. Following are some of the principles of making the process look more effective and good.

Techniques involved in NLP

1. Internal Maps of the world

The psychologists try his best to make people aware of their potentials. The internal map technique is a way forward to make the people fully involved in their making. The internal mapping is the concept of all body parts of the humans and the people are made aware of the concepts of fruition and productivity in them. The internal map is a concept in which the people belonging to every aspect of the world are made more familiar to one another. The internal maps refer to all the body parts of the world, the language structure and the governing mechanism of the body. All these parts are interrelated and they are made more sound and sustainable in this regard. Therefore, it is important for people to make people make aware of the concepts involved in them.

2. Modeling

Modeling is a process in which the subject is told to model the behaviors, customs and languages of other people effectively. In this experiment, two models are made together in the concept and the people have to properly understand the structure holistically. The modeling comes with the passage of time and every behavior is carefully constructed so that the people are able to have a better understanding of the subjects. Therefore, modeling is a tool to induce more skeptic behaviouralism and with the passage of time, the people are able to come close to the mechanism effectively. Thus, modeling is an exercise, which can give proper illustrations with the passage of time.

3. Milton Model

Milton is a hyper-communication model, in which the person is able to have a computerized communication with Milton and Milton is a renowned psychologist as well. The psychologist helps to make the things in a proper manner and this Milton model will make you look effectively. The use of the Milton model will bring communication and character building of the individual and with the passage of time, the individual is able to make things more pragmatic in the coming. Thus, the Milton model makes the thing look more great and substantial in their matter.

4. Rapport

The rapport method is a type of method, which makes the belief of the personality look in a better manner. Rapport is the person, who has to be taken in the making of the individual and this is the process, which can make the individual look more dignified and designated. The ideas for this concept is very simple as it can provide good qualities to the individual.

Chapter 9 Who can be a victim of mind control?

The people that are prone to the following conditions can be under the emblem of Mind control

1. Plain Old bullying

If your partner or any individual in the relationship is trying to bully you then you are the manipulated. The result of the manipulation will come late but the present bullying is the result that will make you go restless and repugnant to conciliation. You will feel that your entire life is in devastation and with the passage of time, you will tend to be more and more exhaustive. Thus, the concept of plain old bullying will be a hallmark of affection for you and you will feel very agitated in its regard.

2. Home Court Advantage

In any manipulation, the victim can understand its victimhood if the person is playing his home-court advantage. This means that the person is not able to see the charms of life in a pleasant manner and he is feeling all bad and bodacious about it. The home-court advantage makes him go restless and in the passage of time, the manipulation gets stronger. Thus, the use of home-court advantage is a reflection of manipulation.

3. If you really cared about me

This technique grants a skeptic though to the manipulator that in order to make him more and more compulsive, he starts to ask more questions like if you had really cared about me and made me feel very great. If you had made me not so uncomfortable in the past and like how you can necessarily give more weight in this regard. The idea of this method is one has to be very relaxed in the confession and keeps on avoiding any such statements, which can make him more and more instrumental in this regard.

4. Emotionally Blackmail

The emotional blackmailing is an aspect, which will have a lot of confusions for you in the coming. It will make you feel more and more inspirational in the coming and hence, you will be able to have a sound connection of emotions with you. The emotional blackmailing, if it is present then it can make the wills look bad and in times, it can make a thing go in an effective manner. Therefore, the emotionally blackmailing is an aspect of manipulation and if it is prevalent in your relationship then you are being manipulated to a large extent.

5. Convenient Neediness

This neediness is the method, which is only done on convenience for the people. The manipulators will be using the convenient card to make the people be aware of the masses of the public and with respect to time, it is mandatory for the people to get to the affection in a certain manner. The convenience helps the manipulators to help the message of their utility go in a start manner. Therefore, if you want to have a convenient base of neediness in you then you can actually help others to achieve the best possible way possible.

6. Killing them with kindness

Kindness helps the individuals to know about the surface of the individuals. The manipulators use the edifice of kindness in a perpetual manner. The people will tend to look into the matter of others by possibly making them a culprit of their kindness and thus, the individuals can look into regarding in a possible manner. The manipulators would kill their relationships in a continuous way and hence, the people will come to know the edifice of kindness in a fair manner. Therefore, killing them with kindness will make the pupil know more and more about the just policies effectively. Hence, the killing aspect makes the kind gestures more productive and potential.

7. Very calm at the starting

The students tend to be very calm about the people all in the making. They make the individual more kind in their collection and the individuals make the aspect of kindness in a just manner. Therefore, the manipulators will be kind to you and if you want to make the best of the process. Try your best to make them manipulators go away.

Chapter 10 How to control people with your mind

The following tips can be used to control people.

1. He is charming and nice

The manipulator is all charm and nice at first. He would try his best in making you feel comfortable and gradually, he would impart his shrewdness. First, he would come in your comfort zone by wishing you birthdays, by giving you gifts and making you feel less agitated about anything then he would cast his dogmas. Once he knows that you will not bother him about anything then he would tell you to do anything by all means necessary. Sometimes, his manipulation is so strong and stringent that he can make you do anything even murder. Thus, this is the idea of manipulation that is started with charming voices and ending in catastrophe. Beware of such people.

2. Denial

The manipulator would always deny any assertion or statement of guilty on him. He would be felt exempt from any charges and would dare to see himself in the crux of any problem. If you somehow even manage to bring him in any disaster then he would just simply run away and would assert his innocence overcharges. He would think of himself as a strong mode of eccentricity and he would deny any kind of charges on him and would plead his innocence all over time. This is the true nature of denial that it tends to be very compulsive and bad in its progression and becomes haunting as well. Therefore, the denial is able to make the people look very bad and obsolete to the individual.

3. Lying

The people are able to lie a lot and those, who can actually conform themselves on it are lying. The lying edifice starts with the inculcation of hate speech and derogation and with the passage of time, the people tend to learn a lot of lying. The innocents are not able to see the manifestation of lying in their inner sides and they do not how exactly is the platform of lying quite degenerate about it. The lying helps the manipulator to learn more and more about the advances of the individual and with the passage of time, he comes one step closer tin dodging and abhorring you. This is the strong crux of lying that needs to be strengthened by all means necessary.

4. Excessive Flattery

This sign is of huge importance to the manipulator. The manipulator is able to do a lot of flattery for the individuals and with the passage of time, the individual can harbor flattery and sweetness among the individuals. The flattery helps to manipulate the individuals in a strong manner and this flattery can be of any side and sustenance. The idea exhibited here is quite strong as the people are able to create an environment of justice and order in the citizens and the flattery helps to regulate themselves in an effective manner.

5. Forced Teaming

The individual can use the teaming of the layers for his own motives. This teaming can be devious in its nature and can reflect many ills and whims of the societies. The teaming can also lead to social segregation in society and with the passage of time, the person can easily regulate its crux in a mature manner. The force teaming can appoint strong versions of impact for the students and with the passage of time, the individuals can come up with strong assertions. The forced teaming could be the use of any strength and value and it could be very destructive in its nature as well. Therefore, forced teaming is a sign of affection for the manipulator and it is destruction for the students as well.

6. Good First Impression

The manipulator will always do his best to make the best impression that he can in order to carefully influence the minds of other people. This is a well-managed task just to make sure that the audience is under the reflection of the manipulator and you will all mean necessary, follow under the trap of the manipulators. The good impression can be very expressive in its command and it can yield to proper potential as well but its lasting impacts are very pernicious. With the subtle use of a good impression, the person can easily establish his core links with you and can make you do almost everything. Therefore, a person having an expression of a good impression in him will be interpreted as a manipulator.

7. Pretending to be a victim

The manipulator is of a harsh and smart demeanor. He knows that if he will pretend to be a victim then all the people will listen to him and no matter what are the conditions his stance and statements will stand correct. He will understand this assertion in a jiffy and will do his best to make the public very bad and obscene. The idea is simply that the person is not able to convey his true propositions to the public and he pretends to be a victim. The concept of victimhood tarnishes his image and with the passage of time, he tends to deviate from the straight path. This mere concept completely obstructs the use of empathy from the manipulator's mind and with the passage of time, he feels very degenerative. Therefore, the person, who is a manipulator, will always have a sign of victimhood in him.

8. Silent Treatment

This sign is of strong admiration in the person, who is playing to be a manipulator. The manipulator will easily treat the level of punishment to the audience and while doing this, he will be silent and stringent as hell. This is the idea of concealing and secrecy that the manipulator employees and with the passage of time, he is able to impart a devious mechanism of dealing with thing upon the individual. Therefore, it is important to observe the silent treatment of things in the public and this silent treatment will actually make the person feel very atrocious. Therefore, in order to see the sign of manipulation the person has to be very silent and if he is found silent then yes, he is a manipulator.

9. Appearing to be selfless

The signs of selflessness are the signs that make the individual look very harsh and strong. The selflessness comes in the individuals either he has a golden heart or is he using the emblem of selflessness for himself. For instance, a boy, who is a manipulator falls in love with a person and asserts her to be selfless. In the moment, perhaps he is vouching for a love affair but in the true sense, he tends to be manipulative. He would cast the shadow of badness upon the girl just to have an advantage of her and even get something from her. Therefore, the use of selflessness is also a quality that needs to be strengthened properly.

10. Guilt Tripping

The idea of guilt-tripping is essential to understand as to decipher the nature of manipulation. In the guilt-tripping, the manipulator harbors the power of guilt in an individual and with the passage of time, he manipulates the other individual uses his guilt. He showcases that he is no the one, who is guilty and he trips the momentary aspects of guilt just to convey his innocence. This is a culture of guilt-tripping and it is easily found in all the corners of the world. Even international leaders use the edifice of guilt-tripping to transcend a culture of guilt-tripping. Therefore, it is important to understand that guilt-tripping can lead to a devastating blow of injuries and badness.

11. Shaming

When the manipulator easily acquires his motives, he starts shaming others. He feels that individual is of no worth and in order to destroy him completely, he must be shamed. He would shame you using harsh means, he would kill you possibly, he would employ derogatory remarks upon you and he would instill a culture of deviance among you. Therefore, the culture of shaming is found prevalent among the manipulators and if one has to recognize a manipulator, then he can use this edifice for good reasons. This is the revering identity of the individuals by all means necessary.

12. Intimidation

The person is able to intimidate the other personality if he is manipulative. The manipulation is a hectic task as it requires a lot of effort for the manipulator to intimidate you. This intimidation can be strong as it could lead to an effective mode of manipulation for the individuals. The intimidation starts with a turning point as it will create more efflux of opportunities for the personalities for you. This culture of intimidation is great as you can create more manipulative tactics for your self but in the end, it will be harsh for you. Therefore, it is mandatory to understand that intimidation is a recognizing aspect of a manipulator.

13. Diversion

Diversion refers to the diversity of opinion among the manipulators so that the people can easily lead to a better productive scenario of people to people contact. This diversity is important for you as it will yield a greater sense of affection for you and in the presence of time, you will be able to diversify your opinion based on a common strand of diversity. This means that the manipulator can use the edifice of diversity just to yield more manipulation and strength in him. This can be taken in the aspect of the plurality of opinion and in many ways, it can be dangerous as well.

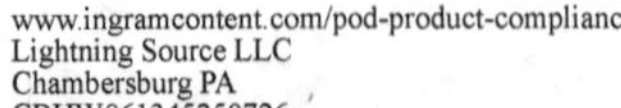